GIFTS & KEEPSAKES

Holiday Take-Homes

by Sherry Kalbach

Illustrator: Kim Kurki

Cover by Murray Callahan

ISBN 0-8454-6563-5

HOLIDAY ART SERIES

THE CONTINENTAL PRESS, INC.
Elizabethtown, PA 17022

CONTENTS

OVERVIEW

This book contains instructions and patterns for 24 inexpensive and easy-to-make gifts for holidays and special occasions.

Activities are appropriate for children in the primary grades. Instructions for the teacher are fully and clearly explained on specially designed pages that feature illustrations of the completed projects. Pattern pages are included to help ensure a successful and attractive project. Options for giving a new look to the project when the idea is used more than once appear with many of the activities. These provide flexibility for both teacher and child.

All the projects have been presented by the author, Sherry Kalbach, in her popular workshop tour. We have chosen the most successful ones based upon the response that she has received from thousands of parents, teachers, and children during her remarkable career.

ACKNOWLEDGMENT

To my mother, for letting me save every
shiny soap wrapper and empty toothpaste box.
And to my father, from whom I inherited the ability
to envision "projects" from those treasures.

SK

TREASURE CHEST CARTON

Everyone collects small trinkets, jewelry, odds and ends, and little bits of things. Here's a special gift idea for special treasures.

Materials

- Reproducible picture on page 29 or old greeting cards
- Egg cartons (3-row x 4-row size)
- Spray paint (Gold or silver looks best, but any color would do.)
- Assorted trims (beads, buttons, sequins, old jewelry, tiny scraps of rick rack, braid)
- White glue   • Scissors
- Markers or crayons

Preparation

Spray-paint the outside of the egg carton. Make a copy of the reproducible design for each child.

Instructions

1. Color design in picture or choose a greeting card picture.
2. Cut picture to fit inside egg carton lid. Glue picture in place.
3. Use an assortment of beads, buttons, sequins, and other items to decorate top of treasure chest. Glue each into position.

OPTIONS

- Use alphabet pasta to spell a name and glue the letters onto the lid.
- To surprise the children, fill the chest with balloons, penny candy, sticks of gum, stickers, pennies, or some other treat. Tie chests shut with yarn or ribbon and have the children promise not to open until they are home.

THUMBPRINT CLAMSHELL

You need only three things and your thumb to make this gift!
Use it for holding paper clips or peanuts.

Materials

- Large clamshells
- Black ink pad
- Black and red fine-line permanent markers

Preparation

Make sure clamshells are clean.

Instructions

1. To make mouse thumbprint design, press thumb firmly onto ink pad. Practice pressing thumb once or twice on paper to get the feel of how hard to press. Then press thumb onto inside center of shell to make body of mouse.

2. Use permanent marker to add eyes, ears, nose, whiskers, feet, and tail (see illustration). For a special touch, draw a tiny red heart on mouse's chest. Then use red marker to print date, first name, and appropriate holiday message, such as "Happy Father's Day."

OPTIONS

- Use scrubbed and washed shells of steamed clams to create mini-mice. Glue on a yarn or ribbon loop and bow for an adorable tree ornament.
- Use this same mouse print to decorate note cards or bookmarks.

HANDPRINT FLOWERS

*This truly "handmade" card takes a little extra time, but
Mom will keep it forever, making it worth those extra minutes.*

Materials

- Reproducible patterns on page 30
- 12″ x 18″ construction paper
- 6″ paper plates
- Tempera paint
- Markers or crayons
- 1″ wide paintbrushes or sponge paint sticks
- White glue   • Scissors
- Green construction paper

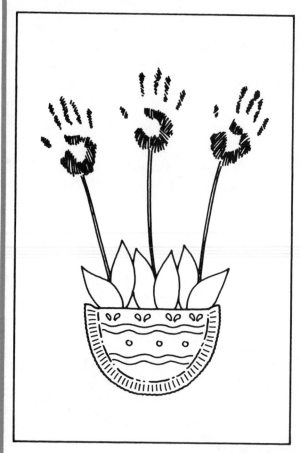

Preparation

Make a copy of leaf and bowl patterns for each child.

Instructions

1. Use markers or crayons to decorate bowl pattern on reproducible. Cut it out and glue to underside of paper plate.
2. Cut off top half of paper plate projecting beyond design.
3. Put glue around rim of plate on undecorated side. Press plate onto lower half of a sheet of construction paper, making a three-dimensional "bowl" for flowers (see illustration).
4. With green marker or crayon, draw three widely spaced stems coming out of bowl.
5. Trace leaf pattern onto green construction paper six times. Cut out leaves and glue to stems above bowl.
6. Paint right palm and fingers with tempera paint. Then press them firmly onto the paper atop one of the stems to make a "flower." Repeat for the other stems.

OPTION

- Print "Happy Mother's Day" or "Here's a handful of flowers I picked just for you!" on the card. Don't forget to mark the day and year, too.

HANDPRINT BUTTERFLY

*Create this personal greeting card for Mother's Day,
Father's Day, or just to say "I love you!" It's a keeper!*

Materials

- 12″ x 18″ construction paper
- Tempera paint
- Brushes
- Markers or crayons

Instructions

1. Fold paper in half to make a 9″ x 12″ card.
2. Hold hand, with fingers tight together, pointing away from you. Brush outside edge of hand (along little finger) with paint. Press down on center front of card to make body of butterfly.
3. Brush paint on palm and fingers of right hand. Press to right of butterfly body to resemble wing. (Heel of hand should touch body of butterfly.) Repeat on left side with left hand.
4. Draw antennae with markers or crayons.
5. Paint right thumb and press on end of right antennae. Repeat with left. Let dry.
6. Print message inside card.

OPTION

- Help the class write a special poem or message for Mother's Day or Father's Day. Make a copy for each child to glue inside the card before he or she signs his or her name. Here are some suggestions to get you started:

    *"Dad, thank you for helping me
    try my wings."*

    *"Mom, my wings grow strong
    because of you."*

    *"These are my handprints,
    As you can see.
    They're very, very small.
    But aren't you glad that they are here
    Instead of on your wall!"*

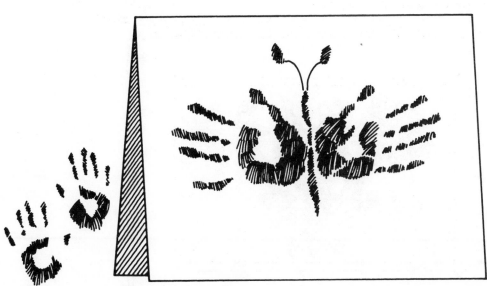

SHADOW BOX GIFT

This project brings out individual creativity and can be done with a wide variety of beans and seeds. Let each member of the class bring in a different kind of bean or seed to share.

Materials

- Reproducible pattern on page 31
- Assorted colorful dried beans and seeds (corn, popcorn, split peas, pumpkin seeds, sunflower seeds)
- Small cardboard fruit trays
- White glue • String

Preparation

Make a copy of the pattern for each child. Cut 12″ lengths of string for hanging.

Instructions

1. Cut out pattern and glue to inside of tray.
2. Using the pattern of dots as a guide, glue beans and seeds to make a bouquet. For variety, glue some seeds flat and others on edge. Allow to dry.
3. When seeds are secure, glue a string loop to back of project for hanging.

OPTIONS

- Glue pattern inside a small cardboard box with a lid. Also decorate the lid.
- Make an initial with one kind of colorful bean and fill in the background with another of contrasting color.
- Small holiday shapes, such as Christmas trees or stars, can also be covered with beans and seeds for pretty tree ornaments. For example, on a Christmas tree shape, a few yellow corn kernels would look like ornaments in a tree of split peas.
- Create flowers from a variety of pasta shapes as well as the above-mentioned materials.

WELCOME SPRING

This versatile gift project can be used to celebrate many different occasions.

Materials

- Reproducible pattern on page 32
- Colored cardboard
- Cardboard egg cartons (2-row x 6-row size)
- White glue
- Yarn or ribbon
- Pasta or rice
- Assorted "signs of spring" (pussy willow catkins, seeds, dried flowers)
- Hole punch

Instructions

1. Thread yarn through holes in cardboard strip and knot.
2. Glue chosen label below holes. Apply glue, letter by letter, to the message. Press pasta or rice onto each letter. Let dry. (Or color the outline letters in the message.)
3. Apply glue generously to outside bottoms of all six egg carton cups. Glue to center of cardboard.
4. Spread glue on inside center of each egg cup and add a different "sign of spring" to each cup.
5. Print name at bottom of cardboard.

OPTIONS

- Make this a nature/ecology box. Add seashells, pinecones, or other natural items. Or fill the cups with colorful assorted dried beans, peas, corn, etc.
- Use three egg cups on a smaller piece of cardboard for a minibox.

Preparation

Make a copy of the chosen label pattern for each child. Cut 4″ x 16″ strips of cardboard. Punch two holes at one narrow end for hanging. Cut egg cartons in half lengthwise, making strips of six cups. Cut 12″ lengths of yarn or ribbon for hanging.

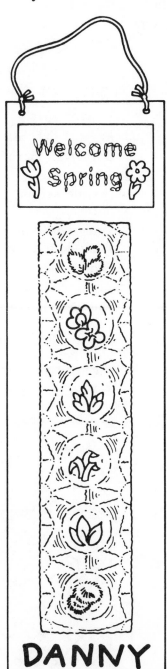

FISHNET SOAP

Something may be "fishy" here, but it sure smells good!
Here's a useful gift for Dad or Mom!

Materials

- Reproducible pattern on page 30
- 3.5-oz. rectangular bar of soap
- Colored nylon netting
- Construction paper
- ½" straight sequin pins (14 per fish) or white glue
- 5mm sequins
- Twist ties   • Scissors

Preparation

Cut net into 14" squares. Make a copy of the fin pattern for each child. *Note:* For safety's sake, have children apply sequins with glue rather than with pins. Or work with one child at a time when using pins. Have children place a tray or box lid under the work to catch falling pins.

Instructions

1. Unwrap soap.
2. Lay net flat. Stand soap upright in middle of net.
3. Gather all four sides of net to top of soap.
4. Twist net tightly one time. Then wrap a twist tie around twisted net and secure tightly. This becomes the fish's tail.
5. Trace fin pattern on construction paper and cut out. Fold along dotted line and pin to soap (see illustration).
6. Slide a red sequin onto a pin and press into end of soap opposite tail for mouth.
7. Slide a sequin onto a pin and push pin into soap for eye. Repeat for other side. Use the same method to form a fin of about five sequins on each side of soap.

OPTION

- Make a card to go with your gift! See pages 45 and 46.

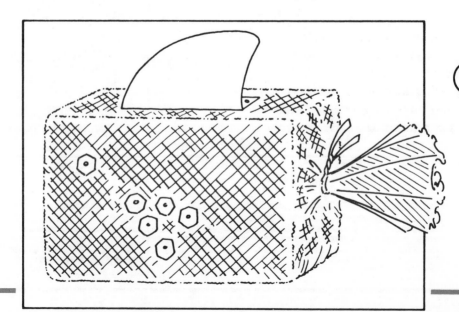

You can make this useful gift at any time of the year.
It's especially nice for Mom! Do this project with a few
children at a time.

Materials

- Reproducible patterns on page 33
- 3.5-oz. rectangular bar of soap
- Bright pink nylon netting
- Construction paper
- ½" straight sequin pins (five per lady) or white glue
- Small silk or plastic flowers, with about 2" stems (one flower per lady)
- Twist ties

Instructions

1. Unwrap soap.
2. Lay net flat. Stand soap upright in middle of net.
3. Gather all four sides of net to top of soap.
4. Twist net tightly one time. Then wrap a twist tie around twisted net and secure tightly.
5. Cut out two eyes and a mouth from construction paper. Use straight pins to push these pieces into soap "face."
6. Cut on dotted lines of both hair pieces. Beginning at cut end, use a pencil to tightly roll each strip to produce curl. Pin one piece on each side of soap head.
7. Gather net on top of head and slip construction paper hat down to rest on top of soap.
8. Tuck flower stem under hat brim beside gathered net.
9. Color card and sign name.

OPTION

- Color the top of the hat or glue on a few sequins or glitter for pizzazz!

Preparation

Cut net into 14" squares. Use the pattern to cut a hat from colored construction paper for each child. Cut 1" diameter circle from center of pattern. Use the hair pattern to cut two 1" x 4" strips from brown or yellow construction paper for each child. Reproduce a card for each child. *Note:* For safety's sake, have children apply pieces with glue rather than with pins. Or work with one child at a time when using pins. Have children place a tray or box lid under the work to catch falling pins.

For an unusual December holiday take-home—a personalized miniature front door—follow the easy steps below. The approach is simple to adapt for any season or holiday.

Materials

- Reproducible diagram on page 34
- 8½″ x 11″ red cardboard
- Gold paper or gold ribbon scraps
- Green tissue paper
- Red sequins
- ½″ wide white ribbon
- White glue   • Scissors
- String   • Gold pen

Instructions

1. Follow diagram for position to do steps 2 through 8.
2. Spread glue in a circle on upper third of the cardboard to make wreath outline.
3. Take one square of green tissue paper. Grasp both ends and twist. Glue to wreath outline. Repeat until wreath outline is covered.
4. Tie a bow with white ribbon. Glue at top of wreath.
5. Glue red sequins on wreath to resemble berries.
6. Glue two gold hinges to left side of door.
7. Glue doorknob on center right edge.
8. Use gold pen to write family name on front door.
9. Tape or glue a string on back for hanging.

OPTIONS

- In place of the red sequin "berries," use dots made with a hole punch from red construction paper.
- For older elementary children and adults, scale down the door to a 3″ x 4″ rectangle to make a tree ornament.
- To make the door for other seasons, change the wreath to a snowman, a bonnet, a basket, or a spring bunny.

Preparation

Make a copy of the diagram for each child to follow in making the door. Cut 12″ lengths of white ribbon. Cut gold paper or ribbon into ¼″ x 1″ pieces for hinges. (Each door will need two.) Cut ¾″ diameter circles from gold paper or ribbon for doorknobs. Cut green tissue paper into 1″ squares. Cut 12″ lengths of string for hanging.

PUSSY WILLOW BUNNY

Pussy willows and plastic lids from deli containers create a very special project.

Materials

- Reproducible pattern on page 35
- Gray pussy willows
- 4³/₄" diameter clear plastic deli container lids
- Tiny dried flowers
- Colored cardboard in pastel shades
- Alphabet pasta
- White glue   • Yarn

Preparation

Place raised rim of deli lid on cardboard and trace around it. Cut one circle for each ornament. Make a copy of the pattern for each child. Trim pussy willow catkins from stems.

OPTION

- Glue a ribbon loop to back of circle and add a matching ribbon bow where the loop meets the plastic lid.

Instructions

1. Cut out bunny pattern and glue to cardboard.
2. Glue pussy willow catkins all over bunny body, except where shaded black.
3. Glue dried flowers around bunny's feet.
4. Use alphabet pasta to spell out name or brief message, such as "I love you" or "Happy Spring." Be sure not to glue anything within ¹/₂" of edge so plastic lid will fit properly.
5. Spread line of white glue around raised edge of plastic lid. Invert and place over decorated cardboard circle. (This will make the bunny picture look as if it were under glass.) Allow to dry.
6. Glue a yarn loop to back for hanging.

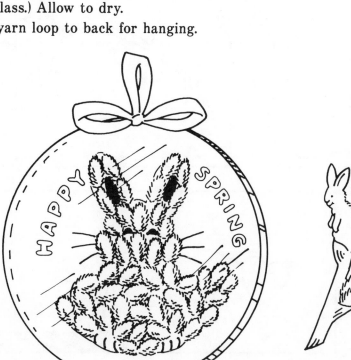

HAVE-A-HEART MOUSE

Did you know that you can make a mouse by folding a heart in half? Try it and see for yourself! This is a clever tree ornament or valentine for that special someone.

Materials

- Reproducible patterns on page 36
- 7″ x 8″ gray construction paper
- Small scraps of pink construction paper
- Black markers or crayons
- White glue
- Candy canes, string licorice, or pencils for tail

Preparation

Make a copy of the heart patterns for each child.

Instructions

1. Trace one large heart onto gray construction paper and two small hearts onto pink construction paper. Cut out hearts.
2. Fold gray heart in half. Glue edges together, leaving a 1″ opening at rounded end for tail.
3. Glue pink heart ear on each side.
4. Color eyes and whiskers with black marker or crayon.
5. Insert "tail" of your choice (candy cane, licorice, or pencil).

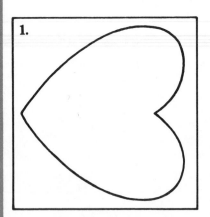

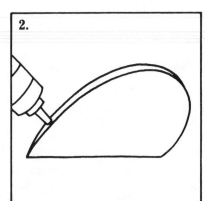

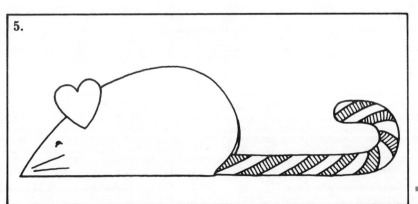

CIRCLE OF LOVE

Create this beautiful heart wreath to say "I love you" any time of the year. See how the heart points form a star!

Materials

- Reproducible pattern on page 36
- White cardboard
- Wallpaper or wrapping paper scraps
- 1″ wide ribbon
- Scissors • White glue • String

Preparation

Cut a 9½″ diameter cardboard ring 1″ wide for each wreath. Cut a cardboard heart pattern for each child. Cut 36″ lengths of ribbon for bows. Cut 12″ lengths of string for hanging.

Instructions

1. Trace nine hearts, using a variety of wallpaper or wrapping paper scraps.
2. Glue hearts, with points facing inward and edges slightly overlapping, in position around cardboard ring.
3. Tie bow from ribbon and glue in place at bottom or top of wreath.
4. Glue string on back for hanging.

OPTIONS

- Use one wallpaper or wrapping paper pattern for all hearts.
- Use another shape (diamond, square, triangle, circle) or a combination of shapes to form a wreath. Adjust the diameter of the wreath accordingly.
- Try cutting hearts from greeting or birthday cards for a unique way to say "Happy Birthday."

Styrofoam packing fill goes by many names: astro-fill, squiggles, or peanuts. Whatever you call these handy shapes, they provide hours of craft fun.

Materials

- Reproducible pattern on page 37
- Styrofoam peanuts (4 cups per sheep)
- 12″ x 12″ black cardboard or construction paper
- 9″ x 12″ cardboard for body
- Cardboard tubes from paper towel or wrapping paper rolls
- White glue
- White crayon or chalk
- Aluminum foil

Preparation

Make a copy of the pattern for each child.

OPTIONS

- Sheep can easily be made larger or smaller.
- Cover body with cotton balls instead of Styrofoam peanuts.
- Try making other Styrofoam "squiggle" animals or characters—a snowman, a bunny, a ghost, or a teddy bear!

Instructions

1. Trace head, tail, and leg patterns on black cardboard or paper. Cut out pieces.
2. Round four corners of 9″ x 12″ cardboard for body.
3. Glue black head, tail, and legs to body, overlapping 1″ (see illustration).
4. Make two 2″ slits on each side of top of cardboard tube. Slide body into slits and reinforce with glue. (This "stick" lets you hold the puppet.)
5. Glue Styrofoam peanuts onto body until covered.
6. Draw eye on head with white chalk or crayon.
7. Form a bell from aluminum foil. Staple to yarn and tie around neck.

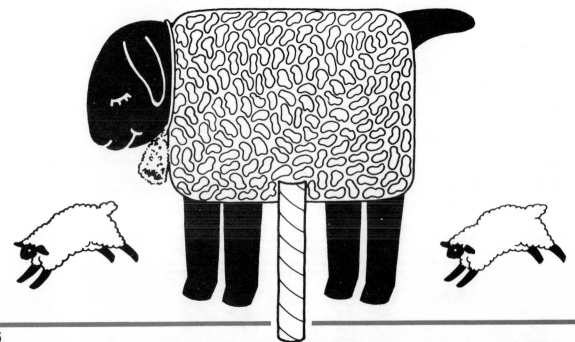

EGGHEAD PLANTER AND CARD

This perfect Father's Day gift is guaranteed to bring a smile to Dad on his special day.

EGGHEAD PLANTER

Materials

- Eggs
- Permanent markers
- Yarn scraps
- White glue
- Rectangular egg cartons
- Rye grass seed (1 tsp. per planter)
- Potting soil or cotton balls
- Spoon • Water

Preparation

Prepare eggshells: Crack eggs at top, keeping lower three-quarters of shell intact. Empty contents. Wash and dry shells. Cut egg cartons into thirds (three sections of four cups) for take-home carriers.

Instructions

1. Use permanent markers to make a face on eggshell.
2. Glue yarn scraps around top of egg for hair.
3. Fill the shell either by spooning potting soil into it or by stuffing with cotton. (Cotton is easier and less messy.)
4. Generously sprinkle on grass seed and dampen with water.
5. When the grass seed has sprouted, the gift is ready to take home in its egg carton "nest." To display planter, cut away top of carton and turn carton over. Set egg planter in center of four cups.

CARD

Materials

- Reproducible pattern on page 38
- 9" x 12" construction paper
- Markers or crayons
- White glue • Scissors

Preparation

Make a copy of the pattern for each student.

Instructions

1. Fold construction paper in half to make a 6" x 9" card.
2. Color tie and belt on front of shirt.
3. Cut out shirt on heavy solid lines. Cut heavy lines at collar.
4. Fold tabs at collar down on dashed lines.
5. Glue shirt to front of card, folding tabs inside card. Glue tabs to inside of card.
6. Print a message inside the card—for example, "This year I'll cut the grass for you!" (Dad's sure to chuckle when child uses scissors to cut the grass hair on the egghead on Father's Day.)

OPTION
- Cut wrapping paper in same shape as tie on reproducible. Paste on card.

PAPER CLIP JEWELRY

Make one for Mom for her special day,
or surprise a friend with a special gift.

Materials

- Contact paper in various colors and patterns
- $1\frac{1}{4}$" paper clips

Preparation

Cut contact paper into 1" squares with backing in place. Cut one piece for each paper clip.

Instructions

1. Hook paper clips together to make a necklace large enough to slip over a person's head.
2. Peel backing off one piece of contact paper. Wrap contact paper around middle of one paper clip, overlapping edges to seal and leaving ends of paper clip free (see illustration).
3. Repeat until each clip is covered.

OPTION

- Add a fancy touch to the necklace by hooking a three-clip "tassel" to center of necklace. Cover each clip as above.

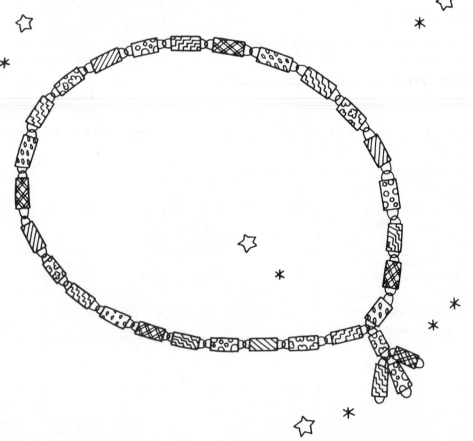

PLASTIC STRAW JEWELRY

Making this gift can provide practice in counting, color or letter recognition, spelling, or vocabulary. And it's fun!

Materials

- 8½″ plastic drinking straws in various colors (four straws per necklace)
- Yarn
- Masking tape

Preparation

Cut yarn into 38″ lengths. Wrap a small piece of masking tape around one end, or dip end into melted paraffin to strengthen yarn and make stringing easier. Cut straws into ³/₄″ lengths.

Instructions

1. Thread a straw on the yarn to within 3″ of its end. Tie a fat knot in the end of the yarn to prevent remaining straws from sliding off.
2. Continue threading straws onto yarn.
3. Tie ends in a double knot.

OPTIONS

- Use shorter lengths of yarn for bracelets.
- String weekly spelling words among the straws. Have the children print words on small strips of paper. Punch a hole in one end of the paper strips and thread, interspersing with the straws. Or use the letters in a child's name, one letter per strip...or words that have a short "a" sound...or simple strips of colored paper just for the color and texture they add! The possibilities are endless!

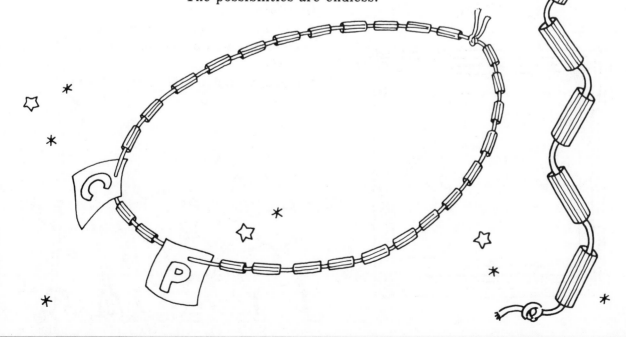

19

TOOTHPICK PICTURE FRAME

This easy-to-make picture keepsake is just right for many occasions.

Materials

- Reproducible patterns on page 39
- Markers or crayons
- Round toothpicks (twelve per frame and one for a glue stick)
- White glue • Scissors
- String • Pencil
- Cardboard • Waxed paper

Preparation

Cut out 2¼" cardboard squares. Make a copy of the selected pattern for each student. Cut 12" lengths of string for hanging. Cut 6" squares of waxed paper.

Instructions

1. Color the selected greeting and cut it out. Glue greeting to cardboard square.
2. Place greeting on piece of waxed paper to protect work surface from glue drips and spills.
3. Dip a toothpick into glue and spread glue across top and bottom of greeting. Place toothpicks in the glue, one at top and one at bottom.
4. Dab glue about ¼" from end of each toothpick, in the four corners of the picture. Lay two more toothpicks in the glue, perpendicular to the first two. Continue dabbing glue and laying toothpicks, log-cabin style, until toothpicks are three or four layers deep.
5. Allow to dry completely. Tape or glue string on back for hanging.

OPTIONS

- Use 2¼" squares cut from favorite greeting cards or photographs for pictures.
- Make frames in other shapes (triangles, pentagons, hexagons).

LACE-UP FAN

The perfect gift for Mom, Grandma, or that special someone any time of the year!

Materials

- Reproducible patterns on page 40
- 6″ x 7″ pieces of cardboard (two per fan)
- Yarn   • Craft sticks
- White glue   • Hole punch
- Markers or crayons

Instructions

1. Color designs on the reproducible and cut them out.
2. Glue one design to each side of cardboard fan, being sure not to cover punched holes.
3. Thread one end of yarn through first hole next to handle, leaving a 10″ tail. Lace other end through holes all the way around fan.
4. When lacing is completed, tie yarn ends into a bow and double-knot.

OPTIONS

- Print name or short message on handle with permanent marker.
- Lace in opposite direction with yarn of another color.
- Use colorful greeting cards for designs on fan.

Preparation

Glue a craft stick for a handle about 1″ above bottom center of the 6″ edge of one piece of cardboard (see illustration). Glue the second piece of cardboard on top of the first. Allow to dry completely. Then punch holes around the outer edges, ³/₄″ apart. Cut 36″ lengths of yarn for lacing. Make a copy of the reproducible pattern for each child.

LOLLIPOP LOLLIPOP

Fill a bulletin board or Christmas tree with this versatile project. Most kids will want to make more than one!

Materials

- Cardboard in assorted colors
- Craft sticks
- Plastic wrap
- Ribbon or yarn
- Christmas ornament hooks
- Assorted trims (sequins, buttons, scraps of rickrack, braid, yarn, ribbon)

Preparation

Cut a 3¾" circle from cardboard for each lollipop. Cut a 14" length of plastic wrap for each lollipop. Cut 12" lengths of ribbon or yarn.

Instructions

1. Glue a craft stick to back of cardboard circle about 1" from edge (see figure 1).
2. Use assorted trims to decorate front of lollipop. Glue in place. Allow to dry completely.
3. Lay lollipop in center of plastic wrap (see figure 2). Fold plastic wrap down over lollipop and gather at stick. Wrap ribbon or yarn around gathered wrap and tie tightly with a bow.
4. To hang, gently push ornament hook through plastic wrap, or tape a yarn or string loop to the back.

OPTIONS

- Instead of decorating the lollipop with trims, write a holiday, get well, birthday, or other message on it.
- For a sparkling lollipop, spread glue over cardboard circle and sprinkle with glitter. Or write name with glue and then sprinkle with glitter.

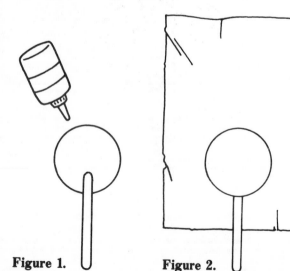

Figure 1.   **Figure 2.**

NAME HANGER

*Let everyone know whose room it is! Give a friend this
colorful door decoration or wall hanging.*

Materials

- 9″ x 11″ Styrofoam meat trays or sheets
- Cotton balls (6 to 8 per hanging)
- Small tube-shaped pasta, preferably ditalini #36
- Red food coloring (one 1-oz. bottle for each 16-oz. box of ditalini)
- ³/₄″ or 1″ wide ribbon in red, orange, yellow, green, blue, and violet (or substitute construction paper)
- White glue • String • Pencil

Preparation

Cut two 12″ strips of ribbon or paper in each color, for a total of 12 strips per child. Use pencil to punch two holes 6″ apart on 11″ edge of Styrofoam tray. Cut 30″ lengths of string for hanging. Dye ditalini by shaking in plastic bag with drops of food coloring. Dye half the pasta at a time.

Instructions

1. Thread a string through holes and knot to use as hanger.
2. Glue ribbon strips in rainbow order (red, orange, yellow, green, blue, violet) along bottom of tray from left to right. Strips should overlap back edge of tray about ³/₄″.
3. Stretch cotton balls gently. Glue around four edges of tray to look like a fluffy cloud.
4. Print first name very lightly with pencil in center of tray. In place of very long names, use nicknames or three initials. (You may want to have trays lettered before project begins.)
5. Squeeze a line of white glue over each letter, one at a time. Add the colored pasta to spell the name. Let dry.

OPTION

- In place of the colored pasta, you might want to use dried beans, unpopped popcorn, or glitter. Check the pasta shelf in your grocery store to see what other interesting shapes might work!

MAGIC WANDS

Put a little magic in a friend's hand and see the smile for miles.

Materials

- Reproducible patterns on page 41
- Plastic drinking straws
- Construction paper or lightweight cardboard
- ¼" wide ribbon
- Glitter or salt colored with tempera paint
- White glue • Stapler
- Gold star stickers

Instructions

1. Using one of the patterns, cut a flower, heart, or star from construction paper or cardboard.
2. Fold ribbon in half. Place between underside of shape and top of a straw. Staple in place.
3. Lightly spread glue on top surface of shape. Sprinkle on glitter or colored salt.
4. Attach star stickers to ends of the ribbon.

OPTIONS

- Before applying glitter or salt, print name with permanent black marker.
- These wands are great fun for a parents' open house. Have children leave their name wands on the desks for their parents to find. Or make wands without names or glitter. Have parents write their own names on the wands and use them instead of name tags.

Preparation

To color salt, fill a jar three-quarters full. Add a small amount of powdered tempera paint. *Do not add water.* Shake thoroughly. To intensify color, add more tempera powder. Cut 14″ lengths of ribbon. Use the reproducible to make student patterns (see page 28).

24

PAPER PLATE RAINBOW

This very quick project produces colorful hanging room decorations to cheer shut-ins or celebrate a birthday.

Materials

- 6″ white paper plates (half a plate per rainbow)
- Markers or crayons
- ½″ pompoms (one each of red, orange, yellow, green, and blue for each rainbow)
- White glue • Pencil
- Hole punch
- Yarn or string

Instructions

1. With a pencil draw light lines to divide the plate into five semicircular bands (see figure 1).
2. Print name on plate with a black marker before coloring.
3. Color the bands red, orange, yellow, green, and blue, in that order. Begin with red on the innermost band and end with blue on the outermost band.
4. Repeat steps 1-3 on the other side.
5. Glue each pompom onto band of corresponding color on bottom left edge of rainbow (see figure 2).
6. Use hole punch to make hole at top for hanging.
7. Thread string through and knot.

Preparation

Cut plates in half. Cut away a 1¼″ wide half circle from center straight edge of each plate. Cut 12″ lengths of yarn or string for hanging.

OPTION

- In place of pompoms or in addition to them, glue ribbon or construction paper streamers to bottom edges on one or both sides.

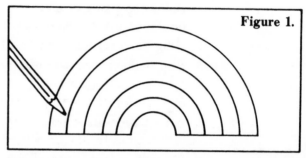

Figure 1.

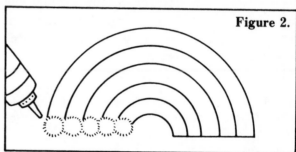

Figure 2.

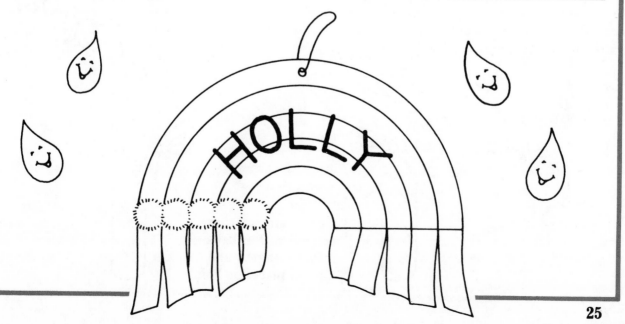

"NOSEY" THE CLOWN

This "nosey" clown is sure to bring a smile to everyone!

Materials

- Reproducible pattern on page 42
- 9″ white paper plates
- 8½″ plastic drinking straws
- Cardboard tubes from paper towel rolls
- 7″-9″ round balloon
- Yarn scraps   • Masking tape
- White glue   • Ribbon
- Markers or crayons

Preparation

Make a copy of the clown face pattern for each child. Cut 24″ lengths of ribbon for bows.

Instructions

1. Color the parts of the clown face and cut them out. Glue on paper plate. Leave space at center for nose.
2. Glue yarn scraps for hair around top edge of plate.
3. Slip balloon over top of straw. Secure with tape.
4. Punch small nose hole in center of plate, just large enough for straw to fit through.
5. Glue paper plate face to top 3″ of paper towel tube. Allow glue to dry.
6. Tie ribbon bow around clown's neck.
7. Insert straw into hole, hide face behind clown puppet, and blow into straw. Watch everyone giggle as the nose grows.

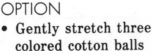

OPTION
- Gently stretch three colored cotton balls into 4″ lengths and glue in place for hair.

TIC TAC TOE...TO GO!

Use these just about anywhere! They're safe and handy for long trips. Ask your nearest carpet dealer for some foam padding scraps and create these games in a jiffy. It also makes a great gift idea!

Materials

- Scraps of foam carpet padding
- Permanent markers
- Scissors
- Self-sealing plastic bags

Preparation

For each child, mark outlines on carpet padding for cutting one 8″ and ten 1″ squares. For younger children, you may wish to cut all the squares for this game yourself.

Instructions

1. Cut out the 8″ square of carpet padding.
2. Use marker to make tic tac toe grid on unfinished plain foam side.
3. Cut out the ten 1″ foam squares.
4. Mark five small squares with an X on the finished ("coated") side. Use a different color marker to mark the five others with an O. Be sure to draw on the correct side so the pieces won't slip off the "gameboard."
5. Drop board and pieces into plastic bag, seal, and you're ready to go!

   ### OPTION
   - Make a checkerboard using this same method.

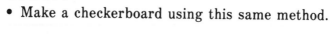

Reproducible patterns for projects in this book may be used in two ways. You may wish to reproduce a pattern page on paper, cut out the piece or pieces, trace them onto oaktag, and cut them out. The children can then use these oaktag patterns to trace pieces on construction paper. To increase durability, laminate the oaktag patterns.

You may choose instead to reproduce multiple copies of the pattern pages and supply each child with one to cut out and use for tracing on construction paper for his or her own project. The pattern title and reference to the instructions page may be covered before copying the reproducible in order to increase usable space on the students' copies.

Information regarding the number of copies of each piece needed and additional instructions are also provided on the pattern pages.

Pattern pieces are drawn with heavy, solid outlines to ensure that children will be able to cut them successfully.

The pattern pages also include additional timesaving aids for you. The basic wrapping paper pattern can be used for many classroom activities; try reproducing it on paper of a different color each time you copy it. The clip art patterns should come in handy for any number of holiday craft projects of your design. The generic greeting card pattern is a timesaver for children who are taking a gift home or giving one to a friend. The open area on the card can be used for creative drawings, or the children can paste colorful pictures or even a school photo in the center. Gift tags can be reproduced quickly for a variety of occasions. You'll find all these patterns on pages 43-46.

PATTERNS

TREASURE CHEST CARTON Pattern

Instructions on page 4

Cut 1

HANDPRINT FLOWER Patterns
Instructions on page 6

Leaves
Cut 6 (green)

Flower Bowl
Cut 1

FISHNET SOAP Pattern
Instructions on page 10

Fin
Cut 1

- - - - - - - -
FOLD

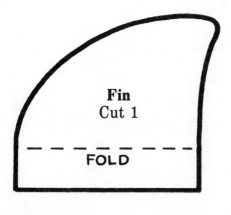

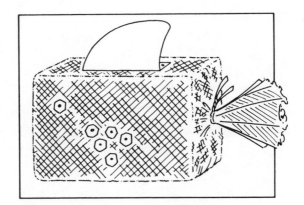

SHADOW BOX GIFT Pattern

Instructions on page 8

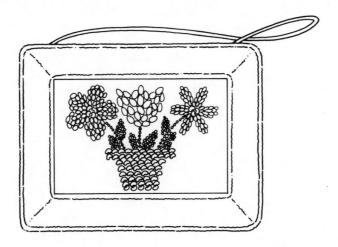

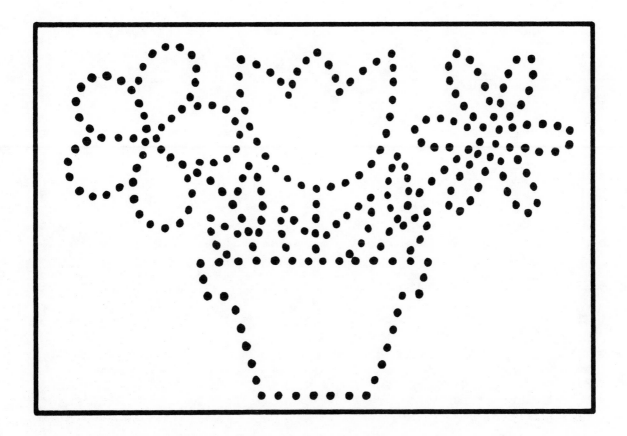

WELCOME SPRING Patterns

Instructions on page 9

Welcome Spring

My Collection

Nature Box

Seeds and Shells

Happy Easter

Ecology Collection

LADY SOAP Patterns
Instructions on page 11

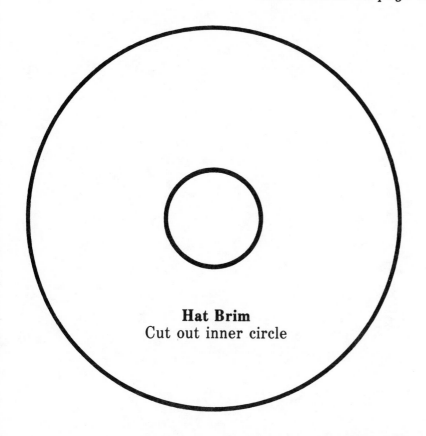

Hat Brim
Cut out inner circle

Hair Strips
Cut 2

Card

Happy
Mother's
Day

HOLIDAY DOOR Diagram

Instructions on page 12

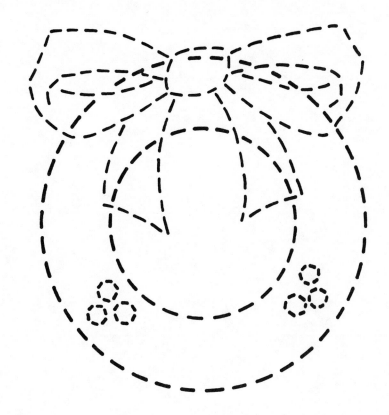

PUSSY WILLOW BUNNY Pattern

Instructions on page 13

HAVE-A-HEART MOUSE Patterns
Instructions on page 14

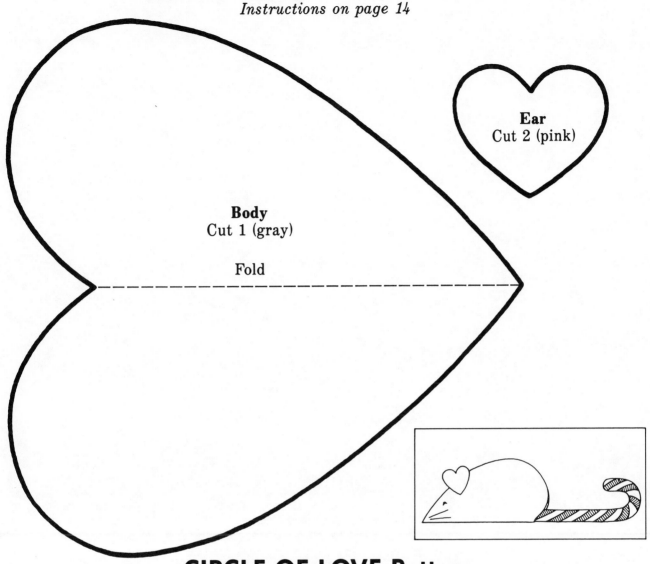

Ear
Cut 2 (pink)

Body
Cut 1 (gray)

Fold

CIRCLE OF LOVE Pattern
Instructions on page 15

Heart for Wreath
Cut 9

"SQUIGGLES" PUPPET Pattern
Instructions on page 16

Head
Cut 1 (black)

Leg
Cut 4 (black)

Tail
Cut 1 (black)

EGGHEAD CARD Pattern

Instructions on page 17

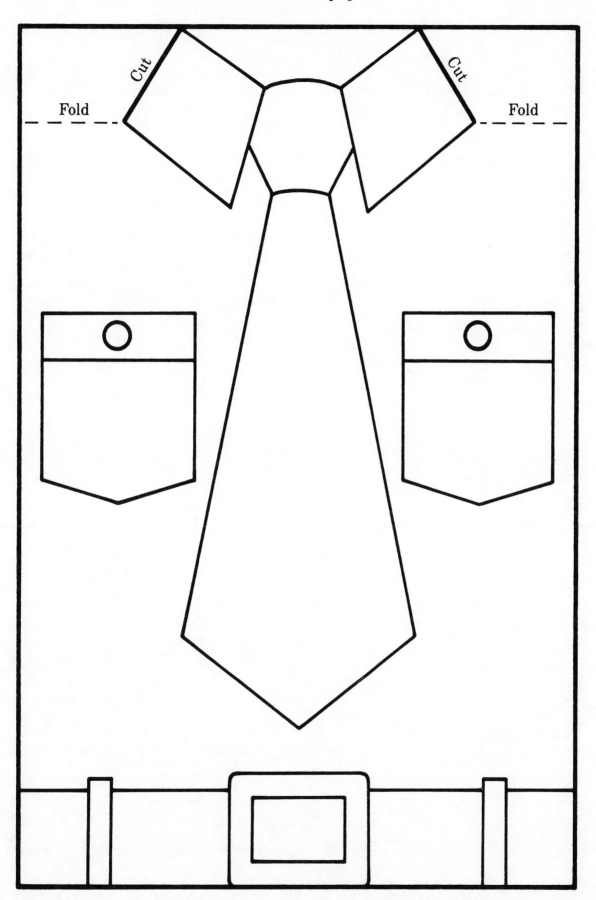

Cut

Cut

Fold

Fold

TOOTHPICK GREETING Patterns

Instructions on page 20

SHADOW BOX GIFT Pattern

Instructions on page 8

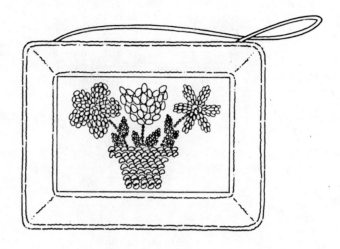

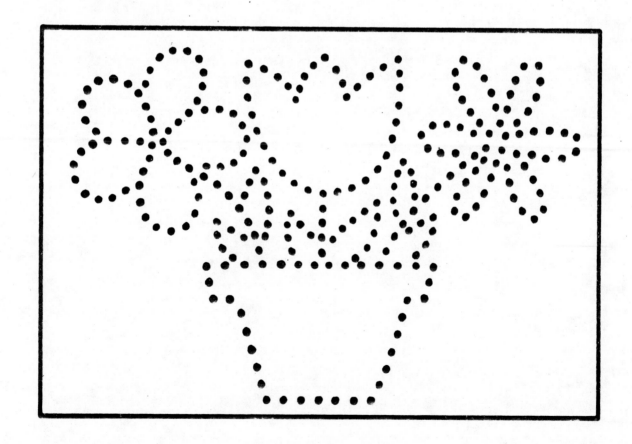

MAGIC WAND Patterns

Instructions on page 24

Flower

Heart

Star

"NOSEY" THE CLOWN Pattern

Instructions on page 26

WRAPPING PAPER Pattern

CLIP ART Patterns

GIFT TAG Patterns

To _____

Love _____

To _____

From _____

To _____

_____

_____

Dear _____

_____